G

by Calum Grant

Lang**Syne**

PUBLISHING

WRITING *to* REMEMBER

Lang**Syne**

PUBLISHING

WRITING *to* REMEMBER

79 Main Street, Newtongrange,
Midlothian EH22 4NA
Tel: 0131 344 0414   Fax: 0845 075 6085
E-mail: info@lang-syne.co.uk
www.langsyneshop.co.uk

Design by Dorothy Meikle
Printed by Ricoh Print Scotland
© Lang Syne Publishers Ltd 2014

ISBN 978-1-85217-048-6

Grant

SEPT NAMES INCLUDE:
Alanach
Gilroy
Kearns
Kerrons
MacGilroy
MacIlroy
MacKerron
MacKiaran
Patrick

Grant

MOTTO:
Stand Fast

CREST:
A Mountain Inflamed Proper

PLANT BADGE:
Pine and cranberry

TERRITORY:
Strathspey and Rothiemurchas

Chapter one:

The origins of the clan system

by Rennie McOwan

**The original Scottish clans of the Highlands
and the great families of the Lowlands and
Borders were gatherings of families, relatives,
allies and neighbours for mutual protection
against rivals or invaders.**

Scotland experienced invasion from the
Vikings, the Romans and English armies from the
south. The Norman invasion of what is now
England also had an influence on land-holding in
Scotland. Some of these invaders stayed on and in
time became 'Scottish'.

The word clan derives from the Gaelic
language term 'clann', meaning children, and it
was first used many centuries ago as communities
were formed around tribal lands in glens and
mountain fastnesses.

The format of clans changed over the centuries, but at its best the chief and his family held the land on behalf of all, like trustees, and the ordinary clansmen and women believed they had a blood relationship with the founder of their clan.

There were two way duties and obligations. An inadequate chief could be deposed and replaced by someone of greater ability.

Clan people had an immense pride in race. Their relationship with the chief was like adult children to a father and they had a real dignity.

The concept of clanship is very old and a more feudal notion of authority gradually crept in.

Pictland, for instance, was divided into seven principalities ruled by feudal leaders who were the strongest and most charismatic leaders of their particular groups.

By the sixth century the 'British' kingdoms of Strathclyde, Lothian and Celtic Dalriada (Argyll) had emerged and Scotland, as one nation, began to take shape in the time of King Kenneth MacAlpin.

Some chiefs claimed descent from

ancient kings which may not have been accurate in every case.

By the twelfth and thirteenth centuries the clans and families were more strongly brought under the central control of Scottish monarchs.

Lands were awarded and administered more and more under royal favour, yet the power of the area clan chiefs was still very great.

The long wars to ensure Scotland's independence against the expansionist ideas of English monarchs extended the influence of some clans and reduced the lands of others.

Those who supported Scotland's greatest king, Robert the Bruce, were awarded the territories of the families who had opposed his claim to the Scottish throne.

In the Scottish Borders country – the notorious Debatable Lands – the great families built up a ferocious reputation for providing warlike men accustomed to raiding into England and occasionally fighting one another.

Chiefs had the power to dispense justice and to confiscate lands and clan warfare produced a society where martial virtues – courage, hardiness, tenacity – were greatly admired.

Gradually the relationship between the clans and the Crown became strained as Scottish monarchs became more orientated to life in the Lowlands and, on occasion, towards England.

The Highland clans spoke a different language, Gaelic, whereas the language of Lowland Scotland and the court was Scots and in more modern times, English.

Highlanders dressed differently, had different customs, and their wild mountain land sometimes seemed almost foreign to people living in the Lowlands.

It must be emphasised that Gaelic culture was very rich and story-telling, poetry, piping, the clarsach (harp) and other music all flourished and were greatly respected.

Highland culture was different from other parts of Scotland but it was not inferior or less sophisticated.

Central Government, whether in London or Edinburgh, sometimes saw the Gaelic clans as

"The spirit of the clan means much to thousands of people"

a challenge to their authority and some sent expeditions into the Highlands and west to crush the power of the Lords of the Isles.

Nevertheless, when the eighteenth century Jacobite Risings came along the cause of the Stuarts was mainly supported by Highland clans.

The word Jacobite comes from the Latin for James – Jacobus. The Jacobites wanted to restore the exiled Stuarts to the throne of Britain.

The monarchies of Scotland and England became one in 1603 when King James VI of Scotland (1st of England) gained the English throne after Queen Elizabeth died.

The Union of Parliaments of Scotland and England, the Treaty of Union, took place in 1707.

Some Highland clans, of course, and Lowland families opposed the Jacobites and supported the incoming Hanoverians.

After the Jacobite cause finally went down at Culloden in 1746 a kind of ethnic cleansing took place. The power of the chiefs was curtailed. Tartan and the pipes were banned in law.

Many emigrated, some because they

wanted to, some because they were evicted by force. In addition, many Highlanders left for the cities of the south to seek work.

Many of the clan lands became home to sheep and deer shooting estates.

But the warlike traditions of the clans and the great Lowland and Border families lived on, with their descendants fighting bravely for freedom in two world wars.

Remember the men from whence you came, says the Gaelic proverb, and to that could be added the role of many heroic women.

The spirit of the clan, of having roots, whether Highland or Lowland, means much to thousands of people.

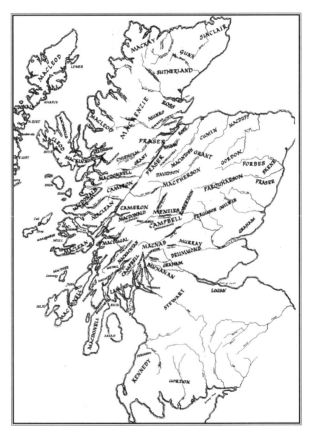

A map of the clans' homelands

Chapter two:

The lawless North

Norman in origin and were in Nottingham in the early 13th century.

The first recorded Grant in the north was Sir Lawrence le Grant, Sheriff of Inverness in 1260 whose son John was captured by the English during the Wars of Independence.

In 1434 Duncan le Grant is mentioned as the son of an heiress, Matilda, and in 1453 he is called Laird of Freuchie in Strathspey which remained the chief's title until 1693.

The Grants were one of the many Norman families who took advantage of the introduction of feudalism into Scotland by acquiring office and land in the north but many romantic myths later grew up to obscure these origins.

According to one, recorded in a manuscript history of the clan written in the 18th century, the Grants were descendants of the Norse god Odin, no less, and were given their name for their grand feats of valour; the alternative Gaelic myth being that they were descended from the first King of Scotland, Kenneth McAlpine, by the same line that produced the MacGregors and this supposed kinship with the clan whose very name was proscribed caused the Grants much trouble later on.

The Gaelic explanation of the name is not so flattering. It was supposed to come from the old word 'ganter' or ugly and to have been given to the first Grants because of the size of their noses.

The early Grants must have been strong warriors for in the lawless north you had to be strong to survive.

Their first famous fighter was Robert Grant who defeated an English Champion at a jousting tournament while on an embassy to the south in 1580.

The third Laird of Freuchie, James of Forres, was another great man of arms and, despite being made responsible for policing Strathspey in 1535, was infamous for raiding and plundering. This chief figures in a story of orphans eating at a trough. These were the children of a Deeside clan wiped out by the Grants and their allies, the Gordons. James refused to have anything to do with them so the Gordon chief, the Earl of Huntly, took them all under his care and fed them each day at his trough. But when James, on a visit to Huntly's Castle, one day saw the children huddled and kneeling at the trough, he was conscience stricken and took them home with him to be raised as Grant descendants and they consequently became known as 'the race of the trough'.

Gradually the family took on the role of a traditional Gaelic ruling line while those who lived on the clan lands adopted the Grant name to seal their allegiance. This process was at its height in the 16th century when most of the cadet branches of the clan were formed.

The stories of the origins of Big John Grant and his Glen Moriston holdings are amusing. His father was a jolly fellow known as the Red Bard and he was fond of other things besides singing if the numbers of his offspring are anything to go by. We are told that he fathered Big John whose mother was the daughter of the Laird of Kincardine whom he met one night at a hunt ball. The next morning a great blaze of fire appeared in the sky foretelling the prodigious strength of the newly conceived child and, sure enough, in later life he achieved fame by defeating a fierce English champion before the king at Edinburgh. When told to name his reward he asked for what he could carry out of the castle and astonished the country by going down to the dungeons to bring out his father who was serving time for singing too late at night. Big John then found the Laird of MacIntosh in the same cell as his father and just brought him out as well, receiving the lands of Glen Moriston as his reward.

By this time the clan and its chief were powerful enough to begin to play a part in national politics. Their traditional allies remained the Gordons led by the Earl of Huntly. John Grant, fourth laird of Freuchie, was in Huntly's train at Holyrood Palace in March, 1566, on the night

Rizzio was murdered and was said to have been foremost in urging Mary, Queen of Scots to avenge her secretary's death by putting the conspirators to the sword.

More cautious councils prevailed, however, and the Grants played little part in the civil conflicts which followed, making their peace with Regent Moray soon after the Queen's party was defeated.

Towards the end of the century, the Grants began to quarrel with the Gordons over religion, the former being Protestant, the latter remaining Catholic and prepared to conspire with the King of Spain to restore the old faith.

In 1586 the Earl of Huntly allied himself with the MacDonalds and Camerons who had a long history of plundering the Grant lands. The Grants retaliated by bringing in the MacGregors but came off worst in a clash at Ballindalloch.

After this the feuds became national and the Grants fought against Huntly at the braes of Glenlivet in 1694. Though Huntly won this battle he was forced to submit the next year when the

King himself rode against him and from then on the Grants were free of Gordon power.

In the 17th and 18th centuries the Grants were mostly Covenanters or Whigs and tended to favour whichever side held control rather than back one faction, win or lose.

Their main concern was always to get the help of the central authorities against the marauding MacDonalds and Camerons.

Chapter three:

Outlaws

At the beginning of the 17th century, though, the Grants were usually in hot water with the Crown because of their association with the MacGregors.

The problem was that the King had made the chiefs responsible for all misdemeanours committed on their territories and the ordinary clansmen were constantly sheltering the outlaws because of the alleged kinships between the two clans.

In 1613 James the Sixth wrote to complain about this and hinted ominously that he would take further action if the situation was not amended. The Grant Chieftain must have got the message for he wrote back two months later to tell the King that he was sending up to Edinburgh one Alistair MacAllister MacGregor who was "a notorious and rebellious Highlandman" but James was not satisfied. In 1615 the chief was fined the large sum of 16,000 merks for his unlawful protection of the outlawed MacGregors.

The next Laird of Grant died while being held at Edinburgh for similar offences. The truth of the matter was that James and his successors were more interested in the revenue to be gained by fining the chiefs than in the niceties of whether there were any MacGregors in Strathspey.

Still, there is plenty of evidence to suggest that the MacGregors did rely on the Grants for help, especially in the cadet branches. The Grants seem to have been perfectly willing to spread dramatic but incriminating stories about their involvement with the outlaws.

One of these stories involved no less a person than Rob Roy MacGregor himself. He became a close ally of Patrick Grant of Rothiemurchas. This branch of the clan had been founded by the son of the chief who had fought for Queen Mary and had established itself by disposing of the local Shaws. The story goes that after two generations of struggle, Patrick Grant finally won control of the land by killing the Shaw chief and then added insult to injury by resurrecting the dead man every time his clansmen tried to bury him.

Apparently, the corpse would be left each morning at the Shaws' front door until it finally disintegrated somewhere between the house and the graveyard. For this crime the whole clan MacIntosh swore to be revenged on Patrick Grant and since he was estranged from the Grants of Strathspey his only hope of survival lay in his friendship with Rob Roy.

One evening, though, before he had time to send for the 'Highland rogue', the MacIntoshes surrounded his house and began to bay for his blood. As his men were outnumbered three to one, Patrick gave himself up for dead. As he was bemoaning his fate, however, Rob Roy suddenly stepped out before him from the forest. Since he was alone, the Grants seemed little better off; but, taking some pipes into his hand, Rob Roy struck up with the rallying call 'The MacGregor's Gathering' and soon 40 of his clansmen had sprung from their hiding places and the MacIntoshes, knowing their opponents' reputation

*The MacGregor clansmen sprang
from their hiding place*

in battle, disappeared into the trees as fast as the MacGregors had come out of them.

By the mid-17th century the Grants owned huge estates and were bound to be drawn into the civil and religious conflicts of the period but what enabled them to survive was their refusal to get embroiled in the Jacobite Rebellions which brought so many of the clans to grief.

Ludovic Grant, eighth laird of Freuchie, set the pattern at the Edinburgh Parliament of 1581 when he objected to one of the acts of religious non-conformance which the Duke of York, later James the Seventh, was trying to press on the house. The King noted the protest but said he regarded it as nothing less than treason and took his revenge in 1685 by fining Ludovic for the old offence of harbouring outlaws.

Ludovic became known as 'the Highland King' and took his revenge by being one of the first to recognise William of Orange as king when James was overthrown. This led to the most important battle fought on Grant soil at the Haughs of Cromdale.

When the Scottish Parliament recognised William in 1689, Bonnie Dundee led a party of Jacobites out of Edinburgh to raise an army in the Highlands. It was this army which won the battle of Killiecrankie but Dundee died on the field and his army split up into quarrelling factions. One of these reached Strathspey in April, 1690, and camped on the heights of Cromdale opposite Castle Grant to prepare for a march on Aberdeen. What they did not know was that a Government force under Sir Thomas Livingstone was camped only eight miles away on the other side of the castle.

When the Grant garrison spotted the Jacobite fires on the hills, they sent messages to Livingstone who then marched his troops through the night, reaching the castle just before dawn. Grant's scouts guided them over the Spey and up to the Jacobite camp where they fell on the enemy. The rebels, taken completely by surprise, panicked and fled.

More than 500 were killed and the rest only escaped in the pre-dawn darkness as the moon went down. This defeat shattered the Scottish resistance to William of Orange and although the Grant chieftain was not himself present at the battle he received his reward for the clans' contribution to the victory three years later when the king gave him the Regality of Grant.

By this charter the chief was confirmed as Master of Strathspey, answerable only to the Crown and Parliament and so to a great extent judge, jury and police force in his own territory.

Even for the 18th century his justice could be harsh. An outlaw, James MacPherson, was hanged by Grant even although he received a warrant on the morning of the execution that a reprieve was on its way from Edinburgh. Grant brought the time of the execution forward but the rider bringing a pardon came flying into the market square just as MacPherson was mounting the scaffold. Grant then took the scroll on which the pardon had been written and put it between the prisoner's neck and the rope. He later wrote to Edinburgh to say that he had hung both MacPherson and his pardon.

Chapter four:

Evictions and murder

If justice was harsh in the Grant lands it had to be because there were always rival clans trying to encroach on their territory and the Crown was always waiting in the background to dispossess weak rulers.

The main clan threats came from the MacDonalds of the west and the Camerons to the south who raided Glen Urquhart in 1514 and 1544.

The Grants' enemies were usually more interested in plunder than massacre because they were so prosperous and made such a tempting target (one castle was stripped with only a bedspread and two broken chairs being left). They were also able to replace their losses quickly but it was plain they had a vested interest in law and order, however rough.

For this reason, any dissension within the clan was especially dangerous. The worst broke out in the 17th century between the Grants of

Glen Moriston and Ballindalloch, the main cause of the trouble being James Grant of Carron known as James of the Hill, an incorrigible freebooter who led the Glen Moriston men on many raids against the more prosperous Ballindalloch. He was eventually captured and thrown into one of the deepest dungeons in Edinburgh but escaped when his wife smuggled in a rope. He returned to his home turf and captured Ballindalloch, imprisoning him for 24 days in a limekiln. By this time the Crown was threatening to deprive the Chief of his hereditary jurisdiction for his failure to deal with the fued so 14 men were sent to bring James in, dead or alive.

Eventually he was driven out from the Grant lands and peace was restored but the Grant chiefs learned their lesson and soon became known as strict upholders of exemplary justice.

The divisions within the clan lasted until the 18th century when the Grants of Glen Moriston went against their chiefs by backing the Jacobite cause.

Their support of the Old Pretender in

1715 led to the sequestration of their lands which were only restored to them after 20 years pleading by the loyal branch of the clan. Despite this, they were only too eager to put their inheritance at risk again by rising for Bonnie Prince Charlie. In fact, their leader was so keen to join the rebels that he rode day and night and rushed into Charles' presence with three days of growth on his chin.

When the Prince made a joking remark about this, the indignant clansman replied that it was not beardless boys who would be doing his Highness a turn. Charles certainly had reason to be grateful for Grant support after his defeat at Culloden when he hid in the heather.

Patrick Grant of Crasky was one of the Seven Men of Glen Moriston who guarded the Prince during his wanderings as a fugitive, contemptuously rejecting the huge reward for his capture.

But many other Grants remained loyal to the Crown during the Jacobite Rebellions. In 1715 they raised troops and regained Inverness from the rebels thus crushing the revolt at its source.

They would have done the same in the '45 but all Highlanders under arms were also under suspicion and the London Government was over-cautious in using their forces without proper supervision. As a result, Bonnie Prince Charlie was allowed to go from strength to strength while the authorities dithered. The Grants were only allowed to join the Hanoverian army five days after Culloden and were labelled Johnny-Come-Latelys by those who had taken part in the battle.

But the loyal Grants incurred great bitterness from Highlanders when they handed over prisoners to 'Butcher' Cumberland and his troops, many of those captured being Grant clansmen from Glen Urquhart and Glen Moriston. It was said they were handed over to quell criticisms from those Whigs who alleged that the Grants were secretly sympathetic to the Jacobites. Prisoners were transported and some were hung but there was lasting bitterness about this among the Grants from the two western glens. The Strathspey branch gained little financially from its loyalty and in 1619 and 1715 they sent in a flood of claims for compensation for damage done to their lands but all to no avail.

In the late 18th century Sir James Grant tried to improve conditions for his clansmen at a time when the Highlands were being cleared of people to make way for sheep. He founded Grantown-on-Spey in 1766 and encouraged small-scale industries thus enabling the clan to weather economic storms. It was probably because of this greater prosperity that the Grants retained much more of the old clan feeling than those who suffered from poverty and emigration.

The last occasion on which the Fiery Cross was sent round to raise a Highland clan was called the Elgin Raid. The cause was the parliamentary election in Elgin borough in which the Grant candidate was the chief's younger brother who was standing as s Tory.

Elgin itself was more left wing, however, and when the chief's eldest sister Lady Anne tried to turn the townhouse into a Tory campaign H.Q. the citizens surrounded the building with armed guards and refused to let anyone enter or leave.

Lady Anne was a great favourite of the clansmen and not a woman to be browbeaten. She had a message smuggled out to Strathspey where her bailiff immediately raised several hundred clansmen to go to her rescue. They stopped at every inn on the way and were a most fearsome sight by the time they reached Elgin where the townsfolk expected nothing less than a full scale massacre.

Eventually the Lord Provost begged Lady Anne to call off her clansmen and she graciously consented and led the Grants home, taking care to order free drinks at each hotel on the way in case the men were tempted back to the booty in Elgin. The still shaking townsfolk elected the Grant candidate, just to be sure!